ZOO ANIMAL FRIENDS

PANDAS

AMY CULLIFORD

T0020213

A Crabtree Roots Book

CRABTREE
Publishing Company
www.crabtreebooks.com

School-to-Home Support for Caregivers and Teachers

This book helps children grow by letting them practice reading. Here are a few guiding questions to help the reader with building his or her comprehension skills. Possible answers appear here in red.

Before Reading:

- What do I think this book is about?
    - *I think this book is about pandas.*
    - *I think this book is about what pandas do.*

- What do I want to learn about this topic?
    - *I want to learn where pandas live.*
    - *I want to learn what colors a panda can be.*

During Reading:

- I wonder why...
    - *I wonder why pandas are black and white.*
    - *I wonder why pandas eat all day.*

- What have I learned so far?
    - *I have learned that pandas have claws.*
    - *I have learned that pandas like to eat.*

After Reading:

- What details did I learn about this topic?
    - *I have learned that pandas like to lie down.*
    - *I have learned that pandas climb trees.*

- Read the book again and look for the vocabulary words.
    - *I see the word **tree** on page 4 and the word **claws** on page 9. The other vocabulary word is found on page 14.*

This is a **panda**.

This panda is in a **tree**.

Pandas are black and white.

Pandas have **claws**.

Pandas like to
lie down.

Pandas eat all day.

Word List

Sight Words

a	black	like
all	have	this
and	in	to
are	is	white

Words to Know

claws   **panda**   **tree**

29 Words

This is a **panda**.

This panda is in a **tree**.

All pandas are black and white.

All pandas have **claws**.

Pandas like to lie down.

Pandas eat all day.

Written by: Amy Culliford

Designed by: Rhea Wallace

Series Development : James Earley

Proofreader: Janine Deschenes

Educational Consultant: Marie Lemke M.Ed.

Photographs:

Shutterstock: Hungchung Chih: cover, p. 1; Galina
Savina: p. 3, 14; Fernan Achilla: p. 5, 14; Jono
Photography: p. 7; clkraus: p. 8, 14; Wonderly
Imaging: p. 11; San Hoyano: p. 12-13

ZOO ANIMAL FRIENDS

PANDAS

Library and Archives Canada Cataloguing in Publication

Title: Pandas / Amy Culliford.
Names: Culliford, Amy, 1992- author.
Description: Series statement: Zoo animal friends |
   "A Crabtree roots book".
Identifiers: Canadiana (print) 20210177810 |
   Canadiana (ebook) 20210177829 |
   ISBN 9781427160386 (hardcover) |
   ISBN 9781427160447 (softcover) |
   ISBN 9781427133298 (HTML) |
   ISBN 9781427133892 (EPUB) |
   ISBN 9781427160621 (read-along ebook)
Subjects: LCSH: Pandas—Juvenile literature.
Classification: LCC QL737.C27 C85 2022 | DDC j599.789—dc23

Library of Congress Cataloging-in-Publication Data

Names: Culliford, Amy, 1992- author.
Title: Pandas / Amy Culliford.
Description: New York : Crabtree Publishing, [2022] | Series: Zoo animal
   friends - a Crabtree roots book | Includes index. | Audience: Ages 4-6 |
   Audience: Grades K-1
Identifiers: LCCN 2021014512 (print) | LCCN 2021014513 (ebook) |
   ISBN 9781427160386 (hardcover) |
   ISBN 9781427160447 (paperback) |
   ISBN 9781427133298 (ebook) |
   ISBN 9781427133892 (epub) |
   ISBN 9781427160621
Subjects: LCSH: Giant panda--Juvenile literature. | Zoo animals--Juvenile
   literature.
Classification: LCC SF408.6.B43 C85 2022 (print) | LCC SF408.6.B43
   (ebook) | DDC 599.789--dc23
LC record available at https://lccn.loc.gov/2021014512
LC ebook record available at https://lccn.loc.gov/2021014513

Crabtree Publishing Company

www.crabtreebooks.com   1-800-387-7650

Copyright © 2022 **CRABTREE PUBLISHING COMPANY**   Printed in the U.S.A./062021/CG20210401

Published in the United States
Crabtree Publishing
347 Fifth Avenue, Suite 1402-145
New York, NY, 10016

Published in Canada
Crabtree Publishing
616 Welland Ave.
St. Catharines, Ontario L2M 5V6